Fishing Secrets *of the* Dead

Fishing Secrets *of the* Dead

BY

Meredith Davies Hadaway

For Janet,
A Godden among us!
Thanks for reading.
XXOO
M
June 9, 2005
Chestertown

Meredith Davies Hadaway

WORD PRESS

CINCINNATI, OHIO

© 2005 by Meredith Davies Hadaway

Published by Word Press
P.O. Box 541106
Cincinnati, OH 45254-1106

Drawings by Cawood Hadaway
Book design by Diane Landskroener

ISBN: 193233999X
LCCN: 2004117695

Poetry Editor: Kevin Walzer
Business Editor: Lori Jareo

Visit us on the web at www.word-press.com

Cover photograph: "The Edna," Tyler Campbell © 1988
tylercampbellphoto.com
Author photo: markswisher.com © 2005

Contents

Three

For Cawood

For the raindrop, joy is in entering the river—
Unbearable pain becomes its own cure.

—GHALIB

One

KEEPER

First, Biggest, Ugliest — these
were the categories you declared as we pulled
the ribbed sheathing from clam
snouts, stinky and obscene, but somehow
right to infiltrate the river's bottom.
My first catch, a nine-inch yellow perch. A trophy
I swore I'd clean and cook, so we didn't
throw it back.

We wore t-shirts I'd silk-screened with rulers
though I knew you'd soon discover I'd
shrunk my own to cheat. Nine inches
on your shirt would come to twelve on mine.
With the ballgame buzzing from the radio
you kept in the tackle box and the river
awash in diamonds, I measured,
photographed, recorded every catch. You
would shrug, re-bait and cast
again. I was, after all, a tourist
on waters known to you from birth.

Later, with your scaling knife,
I tried to clean the perch
still shocked but curling under
the blade. Maybe you knew—even as you took
the knife and peeled away the living flesh
and placed it in a pan— I'd never

eat that fish, never could escape
its iron smell nor scrub
that brine of salt and snout and dying
from my hands.

SKATE

The wind backs down and the river knocks
at our hull. What? I ask. Two
black fins, the stolen rig and bait, a sudden
absence beneath us: Skate, you say.

A second summer of drought has choked
the tide with salt and stained the surface
with this sweep of dark green shadow.
There will be no fishing.

You reel in the weightless
filament. I return to my book. Below,
the skate balloon the bottom as they grope
the mud for buried crab.

Silent, except the hum of another boat
passing, we sway in a remnant of wake.

RUPTURE

Together, in our small boat, we troll the waters
beneath Fossil Rock—a carved-out ledge that hangs
above the Chester's western bank and teems
with prehistoric sea-life frozen in the cliff.
Downriver, on the eastern edge, geologists
have discovered that a matching cliff preserves
the other half of creatures interrupted
in their journey into stone. A perfect

fit, if only these two halves could ever
reunite. We troll beneath the one
and then continue down the other side. Fish
are drawn to rocks as if they sense their history
and their future, both. We drag our baited line
through water, stop, rebait and start again.
How much farther, we wonder, in our lifetime,
will these two shorelines drift apart?

BLACKBERRIES

"I'll see you when I see you," you used to say.
I always thought you assumed too much.

We buried her beneath a tangle of blackberries
out where she'd licked at her frozen bowl.

Your voice dissolved over the phone.
A first taste of silence.

THE VISIBLE SPECTRUM

Light flashes behind black film
and a screen leaps to life—

or death—where fog and shadow dance
like moths around your heart.

A picture's worth a thousand words—
but just the one that counts: inoperable.

The light flicks off with a solid click.
There is no news in this transparency.

Only the world passing
through us, only the fluttering

of particle and wave.

SIGNS

•

Like that deer we came upon, caught
in old fencing. Suddenly it was there beside you
in the woods, puffing the same tired air.
It stood perfectly still while you untangled wire
from thicket. No startling, no bolting.
Just the slightest shiver as the breeze crept up
and the leaves turned over.

Or the heron we saw one night through
the window, glowing like a moon between dark
branches. We knew then that
the world had begun its migration.

SANCTUARY

In March, we drive again through the wildlife
sanctuary, bypassing the groomed ponds, dammed
and seeded to bring ducks and migratory geese.

We travel the back lanes, wooded and secluded, closed
to those who do not know these acres: a tangled
swamp of beaver huts, upended trees and twisted

roots, where turtles slip from logs as we approach.
Here we look for evidence. The osprey have returned
to splintered nests on platforms tilting

over water. They flap from pole to piling, ferrying
their catch head-first into the wind and chirping a ridiculous
whistle, too small for such large birds. They are here—

back early—you point out as we stop the car to watch
a muskrat glide and disappear beneath its own ripple. One
more spring, I do not say. We turn the car around

and bump our way along the edge, turning the wheel
between pits and spreading puddles to avoid
the mud that swallows tires.

PULSE

The heater ticks, expands,
contracts—its pipes
will not keep still. Beyond

these walls the beat:
diesels pushing North
against the night.

The neck, the wrist,
the word—where
can I find it?

RUN

While you lay dying
in a twist of covers, I
went for a run. I was greedy

for death: its sky-broke-

open light, its shelf-rattle
re-ordering of every book
and trinket. I stopped

for nothing as I ran at dusk
across the bridge chasing
every breath. Every

breath. Life is never such a
lungful as death.

ONCE

The young, the strong, they sometimes struggle,
the red-haired hospice nurse had warned.
And now we find that no amount of morphine
will put you under. You just get livelier, springing
from the sheets—a week since you have turned
without our help, a month since solid
food—such strength, it isn't real.

"Once," you say
and shake away the offered arm, refusing
all attempts to lay you down. The struggle
breathes in every breath and gathers
force a final time, one blue-veined finger raised
for emphasis: "Once," you say and hush the room around
like a beginning.

WHAT I'M WONDERING NOW

How the cat turned up on your bed
the night before you died. Impossible—

she hadn't jumped that high in all the year
that you'd been ill and she'd accumulated

ailments of her own: diabetes, blindness, kidneys
failing. What brought her to you

that last middle of the night? They say
a cat will stalk the scent of milk on infants—

was she there like me to breathe
your morphine breath? Or was it hope

your hand would rise from sleep
to rub its length to hers in one

sleek, final dream?

ONE DRAWER

One drawer, emptied
of what you did
not leave behind,
closed up
hollow in a chest
of photos, socks, your
worn-out wallet curved
to the shape of the seat
of your pants. It serves
no purpose but I
cannot fill it—
it will hold
no more.

STAIN

One drop of blood must have escaped
the nurse's needle, for a stain sprang up

on the bedroom chair. I never
noticed until after you'd stopped rocking there

how things appear and dis-
appear and fade. Except

the spot where red wine
spilled in the living room

the night you died.

BECAUSE I HAD TIME TO PLAN

For your death, I thought of everything.
In the fading gray of the hospital room, I typed
your obituary, ordered music, speeches,
pastries, your favorite beer—so much time

to bring your friends around, to tuck the sheet
beneath your chin, to stroke your hair, to hear you say
you loved me back, you loved me
back. But I forgot to plan for this,

this day of open sky and tackle spinning
on the end of my line
without you.

ASHES

The night we parked at Eastern Neck, the Bay
spread its silver limbs around us slowly,
slowly. While we kissed the marshgrass
shivered. From the beginning, ours
was a dream of water,

a summer of tides rising and falling
in the river's most intimate places:
Mummy's Cove, Fossil Rock, Pecometh.
It was water that licked at our thighs
while we waded away from two boats bobbing
 —at separate anchor.

River and Bay around us, beneath us,
as one love spilled into another. Now I hold
you, white and fine as the beach we found
at Jarrett's Creek. Why am I surprised
to learn that all along inside you were the sands
of your own private island?

REMAINS

The weight surprises me.

I bring you back through
the same door.

Nothing has changed.

Following that first combustion
fragments shake out, scatter, recombine.

I want you back.

But the day moves on, wrapping
its thin wind around my thighs and chest,

my hair protesting wildly.

GRAVE

You will always be a body of water. Glittering
with morning, you wrap your arms around the dock
where my boat stirs with a slight starboard list.

These summer days skip across your absence
like waterbugs. Beside me a bridge steps lightly over
its pebbled twin. No concrete marker, only

this moment of surface where two spans
meet: one rising to dust and traffic, the other
churning clouds to ripple.

BEFORE AND AFTER

I mourned my husband years
before we met—a pocket inside-

out, a chair pushed
back from the table, fingernail

clippers right where I left
them—how does the world fill

its empty
spaces before and

after us?

FISHING SECRETS OF THE DEAD

They know about the rock pile
under Southeast Creek—the current's

slice, the wind at Cliffs—they know
this river inside out. They draw

fish like birds we find around
the windowsill, hopping mad

for seed. The dead become
the secret we cannot tell.

They rise inside us like a rapid
pulse, a sudden notion to go

fishing.

Two

GUY GALLANT AND I BURY A BIRD

In 1959 we are a couple of young scientists
scratching theories in the dirt behind his house when
we find a lifeless grackle on the grass.
By the tip of one black and blue and purple wing,
Guy retrieves it, and we conceive
a plot to bury the bird beneath a bush, then wait
three days and dig it up. Guy explains
the bird will likely go to heaven. Why
would a bird go to heaven, I wonder, when he already
lives there? But side by side with sticks we
dig a grave.

Three days later the bird is gone.
In Guy's kitchen, our mothers review the world
over coffee, unaware that we have proven
the existence of God.
Outside Guy whistles softly and sifts through dirt.
I stare down at my stick. Across the yard
on the patio, Guy's black Lab shakes
his massive head, rattling tags and collar
as he scrapes his empty bowl
against the stone.

ITALIANA

Here is all I know, or have been told, about
my birth: boats dozed at anchor in the Bay
of Naples. Trees, their roots

as rugged as the rocks they held
from tumbling into water, released
the olive air that ruffled

my father's hair the day he sat
on the hospital steps. November:
my three brothers scratch games

in the sand as evening gathers.
 I hope it's a boy, my oldest brother
says. The middle nods. A boy, he says, we don't

want any girls in this family. The youngest—
soon to be displaced forever—
has the final word: I just hope it's an American,

he says. We don't want any
Italians in this family.

CATS
Naples, 1954

I'm told they prowled our patio in constant vigil
for the fish the tide left behind

or dinner's bones deposited beside
the kitchen door. One mother dropped

her kittens in my baby carriage. How could
I?—and yet I swear that I remember

this: a sudden blackness where sunlight
ceased to be. And then the light

resuming, the rustle, twist of tongue
and sleep, the intermittent purr.

FREDDIE KING GIVES ME A HAIRCUT

When Freddie King suggested
my blond braids were the only reason
I couldn't join a game of whiffle ball,
I eagerly agreed to let him whack
them off.

What woman has not wished
to be a man?

I slid each braid from its elastic, unraveling
a skill I'd once been proud to learn, and combed
the hair out one last time with my fingers.
Freddie took it clump by clump
and cut it to the scalp.

I did not think I had been violated. I
only sensed that after shedding all desire
to be different, I still was not
the same. The plastic bat made contact
with a hollow ball of holes
and I saw my brother round
the bases.

Beside me on the grass
blond strands swirled and caught
in the bushes. No matter, no
matter. The hair was the one thing
that would grow back.

SOMETIMES IN A FALL YOU CAN TAKE FLIGHT

I lie on my back on the basement floor. Above
me, broken wings of model airplanes flutter
from their ceiling threads,
one bull's-eye, decaled fuselage
still dangling—

A staircase spy too small to catch
the handrail, I plummeted through my brothers' airspace.
In one sideways stumble, I brought those famous dogfights
down to glue and paint and plastic. I wiped
them out.

Lying on my back, I know two things:
I am alive. My brothers will kill me.

TAKING SIGHTS AT "BILLY'S FOLLY"

To test his sextant, my father needs a clear horizon
so we scramble down the rocks where the abandoned
condo project's gate has turned to rust.

With a surgeon's hands, my father turns
knobs and bends his head to the eyepiece,
like a monk who nods to prayer.

Where are you? I ask to tease him, since our hotel
is just beyond the point. He doesn't answer.
The surf is breaking out by the jetty—perhaps

he doesn't hear. Still he bows to the task,
some test of navigation I will never fathom. How knobs
and mirrors, a star, or just the sun can pinpoint

a location, like the rocks that trap the tide hold one
bright fish in a moment of stone before the world pulls on
without it. Where are you? I call again.

THE BINDING

Inside the sueded leather book
with gold embossing, a flock of doves flies

endlessly from printed endleaves.
April 19, 1919, the frontis states in fragile ink.

Two names. Two brown orchids—the bones
of a bouquet—lie flat between blank pages.

NOT ISADORA

—but my grandmother
dressed as Isadora in an album
crumbling into dust. The floating veil,
the long black hair that reaches for her

waist, a dancer's arm both plump
and thin, encased in its bangle, rests
along the slightest sway of hip.
Where one leaves off the other

begins—like fingers, lost
in the tangled stems of lilies white
as her robe, light as her face. Behind her,
a shadow bends itself across

the wall in imitation—a crack
in the plaster running through
those darker limbs.

TUXEDO

Black sleeves and empty
pockets. It was my father's, then
my husband's. The pants

let out, later taken
in. Onyx studs and cufflinks
snapped shut in a satin

box. Cummerbund, bow tie, all pieced
together in a garment bag that hangs
like a secret. Emptied

pockets. Sleeves
that once held me steady
on high blue heels.

FRUITWOOD

My mother had our piano refinished.
It used to be mahogany. I found a photograph
of my grandmother, young, at the keyboard.
She always told me her hands had been too small,
but in the photo, they easily spread an octave.

My mother changed mahogany to fruitwood
to match her furniture. More than thirty
years ago, but it still looks wrong. Like
my husband's hunting dog, locked
in a kennel, across the yard, behind

a thicket. When I play the piano,
he howls a long high note.

Three

NIGHT LIGHT

Now that you are gone
I leave the bathroom light on

to make some difference
between darkness

and darkness.

FISH BOWL

A friend brings me the fish
to ease waking
in an empty house.

Betta, the note explains,
a fighter, who (if I believe
the text) was snatched

from Asian rice paddies
and plunged into a vacant
bowl to circle, pause,

and circle back above
blue marbles. Day by day
I check for cobalt pulse

and wonder: float or swim? Me
or him? One of us will go
before the other—why

get attached? I drop
two flecks of "Betta Treat"
and watch the water shiver.

END OF THE SEASON

White on white, the work boat
scrubs the fog outside my window,
churning up the clam shell

bones of the water, towing
a cloud of paper gulls—the wall,
the sky, to my eye everything

the same color: winter, waiting
to receive the smoke of our fires

NEWS FROM THE FLIGHT PATH

It's not so quiet down here either. Leaves
twist on their branches to watch birds

fall. The river, uncoiled,
becomes a cloud. Someone

holds a ticket for the plane
you missed. Shadows circling

the tarmac. Is there news
from the flight path? A tower

fell twelve centuries ago. Dust
never settles. Dust

never settles.

ANTS

They put murder
at my fingertips. Trailing
past my morning
coffee to carry out
their offices, one
follows another up
the window ledge, always
going, always
somewhere. Even
when I sweep them

from the counter,
they will not
stop their orbiting,
even while I sleep
they are dis-
mantling the night

to bring it, bit
by bit, into

the house.

MORNING

Two deer stumble by my window.
A mosquito bumps against the glass.
Across the river, cars slide past one another.
The cat stretches.

White globes glow like moons along the bridge
each morning. They blink off
and the day begins. I try to catch
that moment, but it only happens

when I look away.

RESURRECTIONS

The waking up
and letting the dog

out, starting the coffee, facing
the shower, the fog

on the mirror, the endless
towels. The tasks: the washing

and brushing, the flossing and combing,
stacking the dishes, the making sure.

Covers tucked, the oven
off. Letting the dog

in. Locking
the door.

ON THE FLY

When a Christmas wreath-turned-
yellow leads a finch to build her nest
beside my door, one

inadvertent slam propels her panic
with such force she knocks her home
right off its hook and flies away.

I find debris and pine needles on the brick:
one egg, unbroken, and two just-hatched
twists of leg and beak. No way

to know if they've survived except the one
who nuzzles closer to my open palm:
a pulse with feathers—and barely that—

but that at least. I re-hang the wreath and tuck
the nest in. Who am I to say a bird won't come back

to a house of fading seasons
and banging doors?

EQUIDISTANT

Halfway down the hill, remembering
how I said that you'd been dead
for fourteen months, I counted.

What tally ticks off hours, days,
and wake-up calls?

On a different hill, the two
of us in the open Jeep,
you pretend to have lost the wheel.

Sick fourteen months before you died,
what strange equivalences mark us?

Blue flowers in a field below
wave me toward you, away from you.

Beside you, laughing
through my wind-whipped hair
when you cross the center line.

REHOBOTH BEACH, JULY 17, 1999

The moment it occurs to me,
the afternoon sky folds heat back
into the sand and a moist wind rattles
the magazine in my fingers. I hear a woman
calling over the surf.

One small child comes apart from a knot
of children splashing in the shallows.
The woman, leaving, it seems. The child,
receiving instruction, holds a wisp of blonde hair
from her eyes, nodding yes, yes.

And then it is over.
A dutiful hug, the woman turning
to shake out her towel, the little girl calling
behind her, Grandma, bye!
and back to the game.

I tuck my magazine into a canvas bag and watch the sun
go grey. This is the day the world turns childless.

VISIT

Was it you or your absence that sagged
beside me in the bed last night?

Clock stabbing the dark with green,
the sting of ozone lingering,

I turned to face your back, to call
your name. No sound

would leave my lips. Only
the rain rippling the roof. Only

the wind rubbing the walls
through closed windows.

FINAL ACCOUNTS

The slow lines at the grocery store, ten pounds
of potatoes, three peaches (one of which
I notice now has turned to bruise), a quart
of berries, an onion shedding
paper skin as it travels toward
the chirp of the scanner—

July 19—twelve dollars and ten cents—two years
since diagnosis, what seems surreal is not that world
but this one you left me.

THE MOON, THE MOUSE, THE SPIDER

Clare, Morgan, Thomas, Rees: I was
a good mother to the children I never had.

I read them books at bedtime,
their small fingers pointing and turning

the pages, over and over again—they never
tired of the moon, the mouse, the spider.

When summer storms shook the house, we counted
the seconds from flash to thunder.

One boy grew dark
and strong like his father. The girl

was blond and played the harp. The others
were babies, too little for language.

So many times I thought I heard
their heartbeats. Now they are quiet.

They've learned to sleep
through the night.

ORBIT

Even the sun comes back
to a cormorant who only dives
and rises—one flick of beak

extinguishing a minnow spark
before the bird descends—then breath
and feather raise him up. Over.

And over again. The end in that beginning
just won't end. The squirrel keeps leaping
after seed, a chipmunk darts from bush

to rock to earthy hole
in constant orbit. You return
with every rising tide, why

shouldn't I?

HERE AFTER

My neighbor died three months ago
but her grown children cannot bring themselves
to sell the house. Instead they've rigged the place

with timers. At five o'clock the living room
lights up for cocktails. At six the kitchen's
brightness signals the beginning of the evening

meal. By ten the bedroom window glows
in case one wants to read in bed.
And so the house—its cupboards packed

with earthly goods, the car still in the drive—lives on
as timers orbit notch by notch around their dials.
One night a shape behind the shade

pulsed and flickered and stopped me
cold until I recognized the random rhythm
of the evening news. Later

I watched a large, gray cat leap once
and disappear behind foundation plantings.
How nice, I thought, the house

has taken in a stray—though I worry now:
is the cat finding food? Is the house watching
too much television? This week's snowstorm has kept me

home for three straight days. I pace from room
to room while the river rises, and drifts
climb the walls. The house next door, gone white,

goes on turning on and off. No one in, no one
out. No footprints. Just a wisp of smoke hanging
over the chimney like breath in the cold.

SOMETHING BLUE

The groom dances with the bride who dances
with her father who dances with his ex-

wife who dances with her current
spouse who dances with the ex-husband's

new girlfriend who dances with the dead
son's best friend who dances with his live-in

lover who dances with the maid
of honor who's had a boob job. Cut

the cake and fling those flowers. The ice
is weeping. Weeping.

REUNION

A woman golfer and a dolphin
trainer on a stormy summer night:
"Don't look back," he says. "I
almost died," she says.

We swirl our drinks. The ice cubes rattle.
Trees flicker in the distance

as the wind picks up.

A CAT, A RASPBERRY

She prances in antici-
pation of the treat she may
not eat, just wondering what

will it be today? A raspberry, plump, per-
plex with bursting seeds—a red
smear I find later

on the counter.

CANCELLED TRIP

Five days clear like water upriver, windless
water I part with one bold opening

of my arms in a moment of float.

CONFLUENCE

How the dog knows to rise
from sleep to trot his

trot from scent to
smell just as the trees

drain the last
drop from the sun and the clouds

close in across
the road where a light flicks on

outside a kitchen
door and the salty

bones of pork chops scrape
against a plate, a clatter of fork and flapping

lid—summed up in one
twist of night and plastic. Precarious

and overfilled, the future waits beyond the curb
for morning pick-up.

HOSTAGE

Even under the red knuckles of August,
I will not renounce the heat of my own body.
I run hot water, wrap in blankets, spill
my sweat, pour tea, more tea, to linger
in steam rising.

Even with summer's finger on the trigger,
fields of sunflowers nod and bend
in prayer. For sun. What else
to ask for? Let the river
pray for rain.

ANAGLYPTIC

Medallions on the ceiling, cast in low
relief, reflect the light from fixtures they surround— a
scattering
of swirls that swell in shadows, white
on slightly whiter white, or gray
that circles into cloud.

Remember this, my father seems to tell me.
Every now and then you must look up.

MORNING WITHOUT POETRY

No breeze stirs the white curtain.
Tomorrow I will forget

the breath inscribing the window,
the river's wake in the marshgrass.

I'm nearing the end of the book
I haven't written yet.

CATCH AND RELEASE

A full moon turns the shore
on end and silvers every wave of night

that laps at the wooden house.
A dock heaves

sideways. Pilings splinter
into weeds—everything

comes back. Even the darkness,
caught in a net

of stars, will be released
into daylight.

HERE, ON THE CHESTER

Wind sweeps the river's
secrets down to shell and mud

and air. Three herons stroll through puddles
after minnow-spark. Straddling rock

and sand, a sycamore drops its mottled bark
on a bank that soon

will disappear. Rivers grow larger, rivers grow
small. Here, where the dead like pebbles rise

among the weeds, I'll build my house
on water.

Notes & Acknowledgements

The translation of Ghalib in the opening epigram is a translation by Jane Hirshfield, taken from her book *Nine Gates: Entering the Mind of Poetry* (New York: Harper Collins, 1997).

"Signs" was inspired by the poem "Doe" by C.K. Williams, which is included in his collection titled *The Singing* (New York: Farrar, Straus and Giroux, 2003).

"Here After" is dedicated to the memory of Jane Learman.

"Here, On the Chester" was inspired by the poem "Rivers Grow Small" by Czeslaw Milosz, which is included in his *New and Collected Poems, 1931–2001* (New York: HarperCollins Publishers, 2001).

I gratefully acknowledge the following journals, where these poems first appeared:
> *The Absinthe Literary Review,* "Stain," "Run," "Remains" and "What I'm Wondering Now."
> *Currents,* "Here, On the Chester"
> *The Delmarva Quarterly,* "On the Fly"

Isotope, A Journal of Literary Nature and Science Writing,
   "Signs"
The Lilliput Review, "Night Light"
MARGIE, Journal of American Poetry, "Something Blue"
Milestone, "Fish Bowl"

I wish to thank my friends and advisors at Vermont College
for their encouragement and support, especially Mary
Ruefle, Jody Gladding, Ralph Angel, Nance Van Winckel,
Louise Crowley, Kelly Lenox Allan, David McNaron,
Barbara Buckman Strasko, Frank Giampietro, Sarah Maclay,
Michele Rosenthal, Heidi Bryan, and Alison Seevak.

I owe more than I can say to my colleagues at Washington
College, especially to Robert Day, Robert Mooney, Erin
Murphy, Diane Landskroener, Marcia Landskroener, Ted
Knight, John Buettner, and Greg Waddell.

Others who have been invaluable readers along the way
include Melora Wolff, Sylvia Baer, Julianna Baggott, Molly
Fisk, Eamon Grennan, Michael Collier, and the late
Roland Flint.

Special thanks to those friends, family members, and doctors
who supported me and Cawood during his illness. They are
too many to name. Thanks also to those who helped me pick
up the pieces, especially John Lang.

My greatest debt is to the late Cawood Hadaway whose life
was —as we say on the Eastern Shore—"a piece of work"
and also a piece of art.

About the Author

Meredith Davies Hadaway's poems have appeared, or are forthcoming, in *Absinthe Literary Review, Ellipsis, Isotope, Lilliput Review, MARGIE, Currents,* the *Delmarva Quarterly,* and the *Milestone.* Her reviews have appeared in *Poetry International.* She lives in Chestertown, on Maryland's Eastern Shore, where she serves as the Vice President for College Relations at Washington College. She is also a musician who has performed in the U.S. and Ireland. She holds a Master of Fine Arts in writing from Vermont College.

About the Artist

Cawood Hadaway was an artist, teacher, and outdoorsman, born and raised on Maryland's Eastern Shore. He earned his B.F.A. and M.F.A. from Maryland Institute College of Art. He died of cancer in September, 2000.

Printed in the United States
29567LVS00002B/58-78

9 781932 339994